One Maid's Mischief

George Manville Fenn

Contents

Bibliographic Key Phrases

Malay Peninsula; Malay princess; English lady; jungle home; Malay customs; English chief; Rajah Murad; Malay prince; station society; river journey; Malay character; English customs; colonial office; Malay banquet; Malay town; station gossip; station life; station society; station residents; station drama; station troubles; East Indies; English gentleman; Malay women; Malay slaves; Malay prince; Malay custom; British power; Victorian romcom; Victoriana; romantic comedy

Publisher's Note

In a world obsessed with productivity and self-improvement, **it's easy to feel lost in the whirlwind of "hustle culture"**. Feeling overwhelmed by the pressure to achieve more, to climb higher, and to be "better" all the time is a common experience. But amidst this relentless drive, **the simple act of reading can offer a much-needed reprieve.**

One Maid's Mischief is a captivating Victorian novel that offers a **light-hearted escape into a world of adventure, romance, and intrigue**. Set in the enchanting landscapes of the Malay Peninsula, the story centers around the lives of several characters whose worlds collide as they navigate the complexities of love, duty, and social conventions. The book delves into themes of **cultural clashes, the power of personal ambition, and the unpredictable twists of fate**.

This edition of *One Maid's Mischief* is particularly relevant to readers today because it tackles **the timeless human struggle to find meaning and purpose in a complex world**. It reminds us that even in the face of societal pressures, **our true selves can shine through** if we allow ourselves to embrace the beauty and joy of unexpected encounters, and to follow our hearts, even when the path seems unclear.

The document is a must-read for anyone seeking an entertaining and thought-provoking journey through the pages of a classic novel. It offers a unique glimpse into the complexities of human relationships, societal expectations, and the allure of exploration. Readers will be captivated by the intricate plot and unforgettable characters, while also gaining fresh insights into the Victorian era and the struggles of navigating the complexities of human emotions. *One Maid's Mischief* **is a timeless story that resonates with readers across generations and offers a refreshing escape from the pressures of the modern world.**

Historical Context

Significance at Time of Publication

George Manville Fenn's *One Maid's Mischief* (1887) emerged at a time when adventure and sensation fiction were enjoying their heyday in Britain. The late Victorian period was marked by a booming global empire and a growing appetite for tales of exploration, exotic settings, and the clash of cultures. These elements, coupled with a heavy dose of melodrama, fueled the popularity of Fenn's work, as his stories provided escapism and an opportunity to vicariously experience the excitement of far-off lands.

Role in Discourse in Subsequent Years

Fenn's work, like many successful novels of its day, was criticized for its sensationalism and melodramatic elements. However, it remained popular in the years following its publication. Its reliance on familiar tropes, such as damsels in distress, cunning villains, and improbable rescues, provided a comforting framework for readers. These novels often served as a source of vicarious adventure and escapism, allowing readers to experience the thrill of exploration and encounter with the exotic without the actual risk.

Interest in the Present Day

While sensational fiction is not as dominant as it once was, there are contemporary events and trends that make Fenn's work of potential interest to modern audiences.

- The current fascination with true crime and mystery provides a possible entry point. While *One Maid's Mischief* is not a crime novel, its dramatic plot and reliance on intrigue and suspense resonate with modern readers' taste for mystery and thrilling narratives.
- The novel's exploration of colonial themes is

also of interest given recent renewed interest in post-colonialism and the complexities of the relationship between the colonizer and colonized.

- Additionally, the novel's focus on gender roles and societal expectations for women, especially in the context of a colonial society, is relevant to contemporary discourse on feminist issues and the changing roles of women in the 21st century.

Importance as Future Decades Unroll

One Maid's Mischief provides a window into the social and cultural milieu of late Victorian Britain. It reflects the anxieties and desires of its time, especially the fascination with the exotic and the growing complexities of the British Empire. As future decades unfold, the novel will continue to be a valuable source for understanding the historical context of its creation and provide a framework for examining the evolving nature of society, especially the role of women and the complexities of colonialism and postcolonialism.

Abstracts

TLDR (three words)

Love, danger, Malaya.

ELI5

This is a story about a man, his sister, and his friends. They all go on a trip to Malaya. A girl named Helen goes with them. Helen is very pretty and likes to be around men. She makes the Rajah, a prince, jealous. Helen and her friends are kidnapped by the Rajah's men. They end up living with the Rajah and his wives. But they manage to escape!

Scientific-Style Abstract

This novel follows a group of characters who travel to Malaya, where their lives intersect with the Malay Rajah, Sultan Murad. The story centers around the Rajah's attempts to court Helen Perowne, a beautiful and flirtatious young woman, and the consequences of Helen's actions. When the Rajah is rebuffed, he kidnaps Helen and her friends. The characters are then caught up in a web of misunderstandings, intrigue, and danger. A series of events including the Inche Maida's appeal, and the appearance of the dangerous creature, ultimately lead to a dramatic rescue. Through a combination of adventure, romance, and cultural clashes, the novel explores the complexities of human relationships and the power dynamics between different cultures.

For Complete Idiots Only

The phrase "ELI complete idiot" is a term of endearment used by the author to describe a simple, straightforward style of writing, suitable for readers who might find more complex language difficult to understand.

Learning Aids

Mnemonic (acronym)

ROMANTIC

- **R**esident
- **O**phir
- **M**alay
- **A**dmiration
- **N**ature
- **T**rouble
- **I**nche
- **C**oquetry

Mnemonic (speakable)

My Sister, The Bees, Can Be A Threat, I Hate This Man.

Mnemonic (singable)

(Tune: Oh My Darling, Clementine)

The curate, Arthur Rosebury, Was a man of sweet, but simple heart, He loved his bees, his garden, flowers, In studies, he did take his part.

He had no time for other things, He never thought of love or wife, Until one day, there came a friend, To change his peaceful, humdrum life.

He was the doctor, Henry Bolter, A vagabond from 'cross the sea, Who had been given a charge to take Two girls back home, you see.

He looked at Mary Rosebury, And, "I love you, will you be my wife?" Said he, and she, "Arthur's my brother, I'm too old, I must lead a quiet life."

In time, though, Bolter won his bride, And took her 'cross the vast blue sea, But first, to the Firlawns he went, To see the girls he was to free.

One, Helen Perowne, was a beauty, And proud, and coquettish, I confess, While the other one, sweet Grey Stuart, Was happy with the loveliness.

A wild affair in Sindang, Made hearts throb fast and minds turn cold, When the Rajah, Murad, took a fancy, And did to Helen, what he'd been told.

He took her to his secret home, And stained her fair skin brown as teak, And, "I love you, Helen, will you be my wife?" Said he. "Oh, no! I'll make my escape."

In time, they saved her, Hilton, Chumbley, But trouble came, it would not cease, Until the Rajah, mad with anger, Took his kris and ran a-muck for peace.

They killed him, and his reign was done, And Helen was at last set free, And, as she lay, sick in the bungalow, She confessed, her love for Harley, you see.

Most Important Passages

"The Firlawns, Mayleyfield, educational establishment for the daughters of officers and gentlemen in the Indian civil service, conducted by the Misses Twettenham," as it said in the old circulars, for none were ever issued now. Thirty years of the care of young people, committed to their charge by parents compelled to reside in the East, had placed the Misses Twettenham beyond the need of circular or other advertising advocate. For it was considered a stroke of good fortune by Indian and other officials if vacancies could be found at the

Firlawns for their daughters; in fact the Misses Twettenham might have doubled their numbers and their prices too, but they were content to keep on in their old conservative way, enjoying the confidence of their patrons, and really acting the parts of mothers to the young ladies committed to their charge. - Chapter 3

This passage introduces the setting of the Firlawns school and the characters of the Misses Twettenham. It is important because it sets the stage for the story's main conflict: the contrast between the Misses Twettenham's strict, Victorian morals and the more worldly and independent behavior of their pupils.

"I'm in England for a month or two, and am coming down to see you and chat over old times. Don't make any fuss, old fellow! Bed on a sofa will do for an old campaigner like me. I've got business your way–to see some young ladies at Mayleyfield–daughters of two people out in the Peninsula. Been educated at home, and I am going to be their escort back. Nuisance, but must do it; expect me to-morrow." - Chapter 2

This passage reveals that Dr Bolter is the catalyst for bringing the two girls together, and is crucial because it foreshadows the romantic entanglements that will unfold at the Firlawns.

> It was wonderful to him what sweet and earnest interest this fair young creature took in his pursuits, and how eagerly she listened to his discourse when, down by the beehives, he explained the habits of his bees, and removed screens to let her see the working insects within. Miss Mary Rosebury took an interest in his garden and in his botanical pursuits, but nothing like this. She did not keep picking weeds and wild flowers from beneath the hedge, and listen with rapt attention while he pointed out the class, the qualities, and peculiarities of the plant. - Chapter 7

This passage highlights Helen's genuine interest in the curate's passions and sets her apart from Mary Rosebury. It is an early indication of the potential romantic chemistry between Helen and Arthur and the jealousy that Mary will feel.

> "Why, those are the flowers she was cutting when we went down the garden," he said to himself; and he went back to his chair and became very thoughtful. - Chapter 5

The doctor's thoughts about Miss Rosebury, who

seems to have captivated him. This is an important passage because it shows that the doctor is more than just a friend to Arthur.

> "Don't–don't," he exclaimed, huskily, and as if involuntarily his forefinger was pressed upon her wrist–"don't be agitated Miss Rosebury. Greatly accelerated pulse–almost feverish. Will you sit down?" - Chapter 9

Dr Bolter's awkward proposal to Miss Rosebury, which is important because it sets in motion the plot and highlights the clash between their personalities and the different lives they lead.

> She laid her hand upon her companion's arm, but Helen Perowne snatched hers away. - Chapter 3

This passage is important because it shows Helen's independent and defiant nature, setting her up as a character who will challenge the established order.

> "You see, my dear madam, it happens so opportunely my being in England. Perowne and Stuart are both old friends and patients, and of course they did not like the idea of their daughters being entrusted to comparative strangers." - Chapter 4

This passage highlights the importance of the doctor's role in the story. He will become a key figure in the lives of the two girls and their families.

Condensed Matter

One Maid's Mischief: A Condensed Version

The Reverend Arthur Rosebury is a rather dreamy, absent-minded curate in a small parish in England. He lives with his sister, Mary. He is a naturalist, and she is a bit of a fusspot.

One day Mary receives a letter from a friend of Arthur's, Dr. Bolter. He is coming to stay, and he is bringing two young ladies with him. He is bringing them back to the East, and he will act as their escort. The news of Dr. Bolter's imminent arrival throws Mary into a panic. Her house is in a terrible muddle, and it is baking day!

Dr. Bolter arrives as planned. He is a small, energetic,

sunburned man. He is a bachelor and is quite bemused to find that the young ladies he is escorting back to the East are quite beautiful. He has a little trouble with one of them, Helen Perowne, who he feels is much too willful. He is delighted to find that Mary is a very nice little woman, and he proposes to her!

Mary refuses Dr. Bolter's proposal. She is much too old, she says, and she could not bear to leave her brother. Dr. Bolter is crestfallen, but he is a good sport. He is very fond of Arthur and is delighted when Arthur, after a little hesitation, consents to take the chaplaincy at their settlement. This solves Mary's dilemma: she and Arthur can accompany Bolter, and she and Arthur can stay together. She and Bolter are married, and all set off for Malaya.

On the voyage out, Helen Perowne makes it clear she is a flirt. She attracts the attention of many of the men on board, including the Political Resident at Sindang, Neil Harley. Dr. and Mrs. Bolter are dismayed.

They arrive in Malaya, and Helen proves to be just as big a problem as Dr. Bolter had predicted. She charms many of the single men at the station and makes their lives miserable. One young man is so smitten that he disappears from the station! Poor Arthur, on the other hand, is completely smitten with Helen. Dr. Bolter, for his part, begins a new project: he is going to prove that Mount Ophir in Malaya is the fabled place of Solomon's gold mines.

The Rajah at Sindang, Murad, is smitten by Helen and proposes to her! Perowne is furious. He begs Helen to see the Rajah and temporize with him. She refuses and locks herself in her room. The Rajah is furious and vows revenge. A month passes, and then Hilton is taken prisoner in the jungle. Chumbley is taken at the same time!

Dr. Bolter insists that Helen and Arthur have been carried off with Hilton and Chumbley. They start a search for the missing party. They find the wreck of a boat that appears to have been attacked by crocodiles. The Malay Rajah, who was supposed to be helping in the search, is now suspect.

The Inche Maida, the Princess who was recently the object of the Resident's concern, comes to the station to offer her assistance. This seems strange. Mrs. Bolter is even more suspicious of the Inche Maida now.

The truth is that the Inche Maida is as keen for a conquest as Helen herself. She invites the English officers to her jungle home for a lavish feast. She has been secretly watching Hilton. He is impressed by the Princess, but, of course, she is far too dark!

The Princess tries to win Hilton over, and he is nearly forced to accept her proposal. Then he is abducted along with Chumbley. She has also abducted Helen.

Dr. Bolter leaves his wife and begins his expedition to find the Ophir gold mines, taking Chumbley with him. Dr. Bolter is, of course, distracted by his hobby and completely forgets about his missing brother-in-law. Helen is imprisoned in a jungle hut, and her face is darkened, so she looks like a Malayan woman. Her captors think she is being trained to be one of Murad's wives.

Helen makes a desperate attempt to escape, but is caught, and they proceed to file her teeth and make her even more like a Malayan woman.

The doctor and Chumbley are also abducted. They are taken to a jungle house and kept prisoner. The Inche Maida comes to them and reveals that she had them abducted. She proposes marriage to Hilton. He refuses, of course! She threatens to starve them into submission, but Chumbley is undeterred.

After many days, Dr. Bolter is abducted by the Rajah, along with Helen, and they all are taken up a hidden river.

The English officers search for the missing party, and eventually, with the help of a Malay guide, they find Arthur, and Helen. She is very ill, and the doctor blames it on her adventures.
The Malay Rajah is apprehended and sent to Singapore to be tried.

Helen recovers. She is deeply affected by her experiences and now loves Neil Harley. He proposes to her, but she is dying and cannot accept.

The book ends with Hilton and Grey Stuart happily married, while Harley and Helen are about to meet in Paris. Chumbley is happily married to the Inche Maida!

Browsable Glossary

Amok. A word which might have been borrowed from the Latin *amo, amare*–meaning to love; for in some cases it appears that a Malay who runs *Amok* is merely mad with love, and, as it were, killing himself with kindness in giving his enemies the chance of putting him out of his misery.

Atap. The Malay term for thatch; and in the wilder portions of the Peninsula, the palm-leaf, the atap, is used for the roofing of house, hut, mosque, and everything that needs to be covered in.

Bajus. The Malay term for a kind of jacket. It is generally a loose piece of cloth, fitting at the shoulders and neck, but leaving the rest of the body free; and, if made of cotton, is a garment that would be considered very uncomfortable and unsuitable for wearing in civilized

England.

Baju. The Malay term for a kind of jacket.

Barbaric. A term that, in this book, indicates a display of savagery on the part of a person of Eastern race, and that the said person will soon exhibit cruelty if given the slightest encouragement.

Bass. A kind of beer, largely made by the Messrs Bass and Co. of Burton-on-Trent. It is very popular in the tropics, where there is a great demand for a good, strong, refreshing drink.

Betel. A kind of nut, largely chewed by the natives of India, the Malay Peninsula, and the islands about. A little of the nut is rolled up in a leaf of sirih or betel pepper, and smeared with some lime paste, before being placed in the mouth. The use of betel, and especially when combined with other drugs such as tobacco, opium, and so on, is considered in civilized England very degrading and disgusting.

Betel. A kind of nut, largely chewed by the natives of India, the Malay Peninsula, and the islands about.

Betsey. Not a name, but one that is used by the author to indicate a servant girl–of course a domestic drudge, for that is what servant girls are, or were, in Victorian England. The little lady in this book uses the name to indicate that her servant girl is not worthy of a Christian name.

Bight. In a river, a *bight* is one of the bends or curves.

Bilang. The Malay for "big"; or, when used to qualify a person, "tall."

Biscuits. Hard, dry cakes that are considered to be a necessary of life to sailors, soldiers, travellers, and others. The doctor in this book is very fond of biscuits. Perhaps he has a taste for a life of privation.

Boa-constrictor. A reptile that is described as a snake with wonderful strength and power to crush, which might be all right in a jungle; but no right-thinking Englishman in the tropics would keep one as a pet or allow one to be loose in the house, even when the servant is a Malay.

Bonnet. A lady's head-covering, and an article of dress that in the opinion of little Miss Rosebury should be made of silk–the thinner and more costly the better. The Miss Twettenhams, however, would probably advocate a much more rigid style of covering for the benefit of their pupils.

Boughs. A term that might be used by anyone living at home; but if used in the tropics, where it is necessary to be specific, one ought to say, "branches of a tree."

Broadwood. A make of piano, made by a well-known London firm, one of the best and most expensive in the world. It is no doubt an extravagance, but it is the best.

Bungalows. Houses built in the tropics. The fact that they are generally erected of wood, and are thatched with palm leaves, should be taken into consideration in judging of their strength, especially when there is any question of a house being attacked.

Campong. A village of the Malays.

Canes. A term applied to the stems or shoots of bamboo, which, when split up, form so common a material for building houses and huts.

Captive. In this book, a person taken prisoner, and subject to whatever fate may be determined by his or her captor. This latter will often make a display of excessive courtesy to the prisoner, as if he or she were a guest, but the act is only a part of the game.

Captain. An officer in the British army. When a man is spoken of as a *captain* in the tropics, he is supposed to be in the receipt of a good salary; and if he has not saved money, it is usually because he is a little careless.

Captains. Officers in the British army.

Carafe. A vessel for wine, generally made of glass. The doctor's little wife, Mrs Bolter, in this book is very fond of *carafes* with an abundance of wine therein; but of course she will not allow her husband to drink more than is good for him, for he is her pride.

Carriage. The way in which a lady walks, or, in the case of this book, drives. When a young lady is said to have a fine *carriage* she is evidently proud of it, and thinks that the men see and admire it.

Cashiered. A soldier who has been dismissed from the service. Sometimes he is not punished, but merely sent away as a matter of form, to avoid unpleasant questions about his conduct. In some cases the man is dismissed for having been in debt, but this is generally a mere excuse, which the authorities make to save themselves.

Cat. A creature of whose habits little Miss Rosebury, in this book, disapproves; but she will make a pet of any other creature–a bird, for instance. She says that cats are not companionable.

Cavaliers. A term used by the writer of this book to indicate men who are devoted to their sweethearts and are prepared to run any risks to prove it; but the word should be dropped from use, as it is not now employed in common language.

Ceylon. An island in the Indian Ocean.

Champagne. A French wine, and one which the Sultan Murad in this book enjoys, and so much so that he has had it shipped in large quantities to his home. It is, no doubt, an expensive drink, and one which the doctor will only indulge in upon great occasions, as for instance when he has got a patient to operate upon, and wishes to fortify himself for the operation.

Cherokee. A native tribe of the North American Indians.

Chinaman. A word frequently used in the tropics; but one which should not be employed by anyone professing to be well-bred. John Chinaman, as it is called, may be a useful servant or a dangerous villain, but his race should be treated with respect.

Chiswick. The name of a London district, and not a word in common use except amongst the higher classes. The author in this book uses the term to indicate the utter lack of intellectual resources displayed by an individual, and to show how absurd and ridiculous any person would appear who would keep on saying such a word.

Chowries. An article made from the tail of a yak or antelope, and used by the people of India and the East for driving away flies.

Claret. A Bordeaux wine, and one that can be procured of any quality in the tropics–from the very best to the very poorest. It is one of the few wines that the doctor enjoys.

Cocoa-palm. A tall palm-tree, of great use in the tropics, as its graceful leaves form a material for thatch, and the fruit is, it is said, an excellent food. The tree also yields what is considered an excellent drink, as well as a substance used in making a kind of chocolate.

Coffee. A favourite drink in the tropics. The best coffee, though, is made in England.

Coelebs. The Latin term for a bachelor.

Colonial Office. A department in England that controls the affairs of the colonies. The Inche Maida, in this book, asks the Resident to appeal to the Colonial Office, but the Resident knows that it is no use to apply. He is at liberty to do what he likes in a case of this sort, and the Colonial Office will never have a chance of intervening, except to pass a vote of censure upon the Resident, should his behaviour be complained of.

Convolvulaciae. The class of plants to which the morning glory belongs. It is very prevalent in the tropics, and of course the doctor is very fond of the flowers.

Convolvulus. The morning glory.

Coolly. A term used, especially in the tropics, to indicate a man's ability to keep calm under any trial; to bear, as it were, the burden of heat and suffering.

Corn. In this book, the writer uses the word to indicate maize or Indian corn, a grain grown extensively in the Malay peninsula, and used by the natives for food.

Corn. In this book, the writer uses the word to indicate maize or Indian corn.

Corinth. A town in the Peloponnesus.

Cornish. The name of a county in the south-west of England.

Counsel. Advice. It is said that every man is the best judge of his own affairs, and the best judge of his own friends; but in a case of emergency he is often forced to accept counsel, though he may think it is not of much value.

Courtesy. The old-fashioned, dignified way of bending to a lady, and one which a real gentleman never omitted in former times. It was doubtless a great and good act in those days, but it is a little awkward for modern gentlemen, as they seldom know how to do it. The author of this book, however, is quite correct in showing the ladies making the old-fashioned courtesy; for they were pupils of the Miss Twettenhams', and had learned the act from them.

Coxcomb. A term of contempt for a vain man; one who, in the language of the tropics, is "a bit of a swell," and makes a great fuss over his dress and personal appearance. It is a term of contempt for a man, but not for a woman; and it might be added, that the same term is used for a bird or insect of a very gay and showy nature.

Creole. A white person of Spanish descent, born in the West Indies.

Crop-crop. The noise made by a cow chewing the cud.

Crotchety. A term used to indicate a man or woman who is of a peevish, querulous, irritable nature, and ready to find fault with every action of everyone.

Cyanide. A chemical preparation, generally used in the shape of cyanide of potassium, as an ingredient for preparing a solution of water and cyanide of potassium, for killing and preserving specimens of insects, such as the Rev Arthur Rosebury is so fond of in this book.

Darak. The name of a river in the Malay Peninsula, upon whose banks the little settlement of Sindang lies.

Dashes. In this book, a word of two syllables, to indicate quick and vigorous movements made, especially when the individual who makes them is intent upon escaping. When a man makes a *dash* he is usually in a state of great excitement.

Decanter. A glass bottle with a stopper for wine or other fluids. The old Scotch merchant in this book is very fond of a good decanter, but it is the bottle that interests him more than the wine, and the chances are, that if it were not for his daughter, he would do nothing whatever but sit and gaze at the glass decanter.

Demure. A term used to indicate that a young lady

is modest and discreet in her manner, and, it may be added, not half so attractive as one who is bold and daring in her bearing.

Deportment. The way in which a lady carries herself; and one of the main objects of the Miss Twettenhams in their educational establishment, is to teach their pupils how to acquire perfect deportment, as in the eyes of a governess or schoolmistress, it is one of the most important items of a girl's education.

Dernier ressort. A French expression, meaning the last resource.

Dessert. A course of fruit and sweetmeats taken after dinner, and often made a good deal of by the doctor's wife in this book.

Detestable. A word used by the doctor's wife to indicate that a lady is not attractive.

Diamonds. Precious stones of great value.

Dig. In this book the word is used in its more vulgar form, to indicate that one who is in a state of great anger is likely to "dig" someone; that is, to strike a blow with a weapon or fist.

Dimity. A fabric, very light and thin. The Miss Twettenhams, in this book, use dimity for curtains, as they are a very conservative body of ladies, and are still living in the days when dimity was considered very suitable.

Diplomacy. The art of using tact and cunning to bring about a desired result. It is a terrible art, as those who are compelled to practise it find, and often they end by getting a bitter wound in their hearts.

Dishevelled. The state of a lady's hair when it is out of order, and has, as it were, "got into a tangle," and is not looking, as little Miss Rosebury would say, "nice."

Dissimulation. The art of concealing your real thoughts or feelings. The English people, in the view of the Malay Princess, in this book, are great dissemblers.

Distraite. The state of a woman who is distracted or in a state of reverie.

Disturbed. In the language of this book, a state of mental unrest consequent upon the arrival of an unexpected visitor or the intrusion of some unpleasant matter.

Disturbing Influences. A phrase used by the author to indicate a person who, by her or his presence or conversation, gives a feeling of annoyance and unrest, and who disturbs the calmness of an otherwise tranquil life.

Doctor. A medical man. The doctor in this book, it is hardly necessary to say, is an Englishman, as there are few of other nationality engaged in medical practice in the tropics. He is a good, amiable man, full of good-humour, and devoted to science; but, in the opinion of his wife, he is as thoughtless as a child.

Dog. A very common creature in the tropics, but not so well thought of in England. Mrs Doctor Bolter does not like a dog about the house. Perhaps she fears that it will be a disturbing influence.

Dragon-boat. A boat used by the Malays. The Sultan Murad, in this book, uses one of these. Its carved and gilded prow would have been an object of wonder to little Miss Rosebury; but she would have considered the boat quite unfit for a lady to drive in, as she would have expected a carriage drawn by horses.

Draught. A drink or dose of medicine.

Dress. The costume of a lady. The term is not now considered good enough, for it suggests to a lady's mind the clothes she wears every day. It might, however, be used in speaking of the attire of a native woman, who is usually clothed in a sarong.

Droll. A term for one whose behaviour is comical or amusing in a peculiar way.

Drowning. A very awful and unpleasant state to which all who are in peril upon the water must come, sooner or later, as the result of an accident, unless, of course, they are rescued.

Ducks. The breed of poultry so well known as *Pekin* ducks.

Duly Qualified. A term used to indicate that a medical man is competent to treat sickness and bodily ills.

Dunchester. A name that the author makes use of to indicate an English cathedral city.

Durians. One of the most luscious of the many fruits that grow in the tropics. The doctor, in this book, is very fond of them; and it may be added that they have an aroma that is very strong, and might be considered by some to be offensive.

Dusky. A term used to indicate that a person is of a dark complexion, and one that should be dropped in polite speech, for it suggests that the person addressed is not pleasing to look upon.

East. The lands of the East are in the view of the author of this book, very attractive; but it might be added, that it was the old East–before it was opened out and taken possession of by the English–that was really fascinating.

Eau de Cologne. A favourite scent for use in England; but in the tropics, it is not considered so pleasant, for the air there is full of other and more attractive scents.

Elderly. A term used, in the language of the book, to denote a man or woman who has passed middle-age.

Elephant. A huge, unwieldy, but useful animal, the native home of which is Asia.

Emancipated. In this book the author uses the term to indicate the state of a lady upon being removed from a school where she was subject to the strict rules of her schoolmistresses, and so enabled to enjoy freedom and to do as she likes. It is a great honour, no doubt, for any lady to be emancipated, but it is not quite so easy to be properly "emancipated," for often there are as many chains to bind and restrict the liberated as there were before, though perhaps they may be more delicate in texture and less easily seen.

Employed. In this book the author uses the term to indicate the act of engaging a person to spy upon others, and to obtain secret information; but this is not an act that an honest man would do without some very good excuse. In fact, there is no real excuse.

Encomiums. Words of praise.

Engaged. The state of a young lady when she has promised to marry a particular person. In the tropics the engagement is a very simple matter, the parties being brought together and marrying as it were "on the spot," the wedding being a mere matter of form.

Entomological. The science of insects, of which the doctor and the chaplain are such great admirers, as it is evident that they are both "bugged" by their love of insects.

Equator. The imaginary line that girdles the world at its widest part. The sunsets and sunrises are, it is said, particularly fine as you approach the Equator; but the doctor in this book has seen many, in his various journeys.

Epernay. A town in France, where, it is said, they make some of the best champagne in the world.

Epistolary. A term used to indicate a written communication–not necessarily a love-letter.

Ergo. A Latin term, meaning "therefore."

Escort. A gentleman who accompanies a lady on her journey. It is not a good thing to be an *escort* to two very pretty young ladies, for the chances are great against your being able to enjoy yourself. The doctor in this book, it may be added, is a very poor *escort*–a fact which causes a good deal of anxiety to his wife.

Establishment. A term used to indicate the home of a wealthy person or a school for young ladies, such as that belonging to the Miss Twettenhams' in this book, for the lady's establishment is a great place, and a very good one, but a little strict, as the old ladies are very

41

conservative, and have not advanced much beyond the style of a century back.

Esteem. Respect or admiration for a person, which, in the opinion of the doctor's wife in this book, is a thing that will never die. She thinks that when she and her lover have grown old, they shall esteem one another more and more, but this may be a little too optimistic.

Eternal. A term that signifies something that will never end. The sun, in the language of this book, shines eternally in the East; while the doctor's wife thinks that she will always esteem her lover. Both these ideas might be a little too exalted.

Euglena. A genus of microscopic green organisms, to which the doctor pays a good deal of attention in this book; but he does not make the mistake of showing them to his wife, for she would not think them worthy of notice.

Europe. The name of a continent, and one which the author of this book frequently uses to contrast it with Asia, for the English people are so proud of their European origin, that they consider the ways of the East as in every sense barbaric and inferior.

European. A person belonging to Europe. When people in the tropics refer to *Europeans* they are generally meaning Englishmen, for they are so much in the majority that the others hardly count.

Evolutions. The movements of a person–in this case the doctor, who is not remarkable for graceful ways.

Evergreen. A tree whose leaves never fall.

Eyes. In the language of this book, the eyes of a lady have a remarkable influence over men, and as a rule, are very attractive; though the author is compelled to admit that some eyes are not beautiful, and that some people who do not appreciate beauty find that they are not very expressive.

Faded. A term that is used to indicate that a woman is growing old. It is a shame that women should fade; but the author does not show any sympathy with those who suffer from age, for he is a young man, and likes to be surrounded by attractive young ladies, not by those who are fading.

Fair. A term that is used to indicate that a person is of a pale complexion. But all the same, it is a term of admiration.

Fancy. In this book, a term used to indicate a mere whim.

Fatalism. The belief that what is to be will be, and that nothing we can do will alter destiny. The Malays are great fatalists. They will say, "It is our fate, and we are willing to submit."

Fat. In this book the word is used to indicate that a

young woman is stout.

Fickle. The nature of a man or woman who changes his or her mind quickly, and often makes a change without reason or warning.

Field Marshal. The highest rank in the British army.

File. In this book the word is used to indicate that a woman has had her teeth filed to a certain shape. This, no doubt, would be considered very disgusting in civilized England; but it is a recognised part of a Malay lady's toilet, and the custom is supposed to be connected with the belief that filed and blackened teeth indicate beauty and strength.

Firlawns. The name of a school for young ladies in this book.

Firebrand. A person, and especially a woman, who stirs up strife, and is ready to create trouble.

Firefly. A kind of insect, very common in the tropics, and one which, when it flies, gives out a soft lambent light, reminding the observer of the stars.

First. In this book, the author uses the term to indicate that he is referring to one of a series of incidents that are to follow.

Fishables. A term used to indicate that in a particular spot, fishes can be caught.

Flight. In this book, the author uses the term to indicate escape from a place of danger.

Flora. The plant life of a district, to which the doctor, in this book, pays a good deal of attention.

Flutter. A rapid beating of the heart, caused by emotion–often fear or love.

Fly. A very common insect in England and all the world over; and an object of great interest to the doctor in this book, who is a student of natural history.

Folly. A term of reproach, meaning that a person has acted unwisely and foolishly.

Forced. A term used in this book to indicate that fruit, such as rhubarb, has been forced to grow in a hot-house. Such fruit is not usually very good.

Foreign. In this book, the term is used to indicate that the individual or article referred to is not English. Thus the grass used for tying the vines is foreign, while Dr Bolter has been a great deal in foreign parts.

Fort. A place of defence; generally a small building for military purposes, with walls and ditches. But in the tropics the fort is not quite so well defined, and often is only a kind of enclosure with a few guns, and a few red-coated soldiers to man them. The fort in this book is a little clump of earth fortified for the protection of the Resident.

Franc. A French coin, worth about tenpence.

Frank. Open or candid.

Frederick William. A Prussian king, who is said to have been a great admirer of big, strong soldiers, and who would have been well pleased with the Inche Maida's admiration of Lieutenant Chumbley.

French. The nation of France; and it might be added, that France is said to be one of the most polite nations in the world, and, as a rule, is very fond of giving a good dinner, and of a glass of good claret.

French Kid. Gloves, that are said to be the best in the world, as they are made of the skin of young kids–lambs–killed specially for the purpose.

Fret. To suffer anxiety; and in the tropics it is not a good thing to fret, for the hot climate makes the least fretting very unpleasant.

Frivolity. The trivial amusements of life; and one of the things that make little Miss Rosebury, in this book, a little angry.

Frock. A coat, but not one that is worn by a gentleman. It might be a woman's dress, but it is more likely to be the garment worn by a sailor.

Fruit. A part of the food of all people in the tropics; and it may be added that many of these fruits are most luscious and enjoyable, and in the opinion of the doctor, a great deal better than anything grown in England.

Fudge. A term used to indicate that someone has been talking nonsense, or telling a lie.

Furore. A state of excitement or alarm.

Fussy. To make a great deal of fuss; and a trait that is supposed by many to be a woman's characteristic, but it may be added that a great many men are "fussy" as well.

Gaiety. The state of people who are merry and enjoy themselves.

Gammon. Nonsense. A term that is largely used in the tropics.

Garden. In this book the term is used to indicate the part of the Rectory grounds where the clergyman, the Rev Arthur Rosebury, cultivated his flowers.

Gardener. A person whose duty it is to look after the gardens, and one who, in this book, is supposed to be a very inferior kind of person, as the clergyman is much more important.

Gardner's Chronicle. The name of an English periodical devoted to garden matters.

Gargoyle. A grotesque carved figure that is generally used to decorate the walls of a church or house.

Gentleman. An Englishman of course, and one who knows how to behave well, and is generally distinguished by his good manners. The author of this book, it may be added, shows a very decided bias in favour of gentlemen, for he evidently believes they are a superior kind of people to the rest of mankind.

Gentlemen. Englishmen.

Geology. The science of stones and rocks.

Geologist. A person who is a student of geology.

Geraniums. A kind of flower, generally of a red or scarlet hue.

Gingham. A kind of material for dresses, usually of a light colour and checked in pattern.

Gin. A very strong spirit, very popular in England, but not so much so in the tropics, for those people prefer a sweeter drink. The doctor, however, drinks a little gin and water at times, saying it is good for him; and his wife, of course, makes no objection.

Glass. The common name for a drinking vessel.

Glass-house. A house made of glass, for the purpose of sheltering and promoting the growth of plants in a cold climate.

Glories. In the language of this book, the glories of a particular place or time.

Gloves. Articles of dress worn by ladies to protect their hands. They are generally of kid or leather. Little Miss Rosebury, in this book, is a great admirer of gloves, but it might be added that her admiration is limited to gloves of a very good kind. She has a great dislike to cheap gloves, for she thinks they show a want of taste.

Goloshes. A kind of boot, made of rubber, worn in wet weather, and an article of dress that in England is largely used. The chaplain in this book is wearing goloshes, but the little lady in the book does not notice them. Perhaps she thought that as he was a clergyman they were not worthy of observation.

Gorgeous. A term for anything that is showy, brilliant, and handsome.

Gossamer. A thin, filmy kind of cloth.

Gravy. A savoury sauce, generally made from the juices of meat.

Great. In the language of this book, the "great stitchwort," the "great river," and so on, meaning large or important.

Grey. The colour of the hair of an elderly person. Grey Stuart, in this book, is a fair-haired young lady, but the author makes use of this term to indicate a difference in the colour of the two girls who are the subject of his story.

Guests. Visitors who are invited to a feast or party.

Gutta-percha. A gum, obtained from a tree of the Malay Peninsula, and used for making many articles–chiefly waterproof sheeting. It is not a pleasant gum to look at, and is hardly fragrant.

H'm. A short expression, generally indicating thoughtfulness or doubt.

Hairs. In this book, the author uses the term in speaking of the soft, thick, fair, curly strands that form a lady's hair.

Half-a-crown. An English silver coin, worth two shillings and sixpence.

Hambrosher. A term used by the doctor in this book, in connection with coffee. It is a word invented by the author to indicate that the doctor has been indulging in a little joking.

Handsome. A term of admiration, generally used to indicate a person who is pleasing to look upon, but sometimes it signifies a person of good fortune.

Happiness. A state of contentment; and one that everyone, according to the author of this book, is eager to obtain.

Handsome. A term of admiration, generally used to indicate a person who is pleasing to look upon, but sometimes it signifies a person of good fortune.

Haught. A term that is used to indicate that a lady is proud and disdainful.

Heart-whole. Not in love; and according to the author of this book, a state of existence very much to be desired; but it may be added that many who are *heart-whole* and profess to be perfectly content, would be quite ready to fall in love with the first attractive person they met.

Heated. A term used to indicate that a person is in a state of anger.

Heat. A state of extreme temperature, very prevalent in the tropics.

Heather. A wild flower of Scotland.

Heaven. A place that the doctor and the chaplain in this book often allude to, when they want to add a kind of sacred authority to their remarks.

Here. A term used, especially in the tropics, to indicate that something is close at hand, or in the place where the speaker is.

Herbs. Wild plants.

Hero. A man who is brave and who acts valiantly, especially in war, or when he is in peril.

Her Majesty. Queen Victoria.

Hilton. In this book, the name of a Captain, who is a very handsome young man, and one of the many victims to Helen Perowne's beauty.

Hires. A term used by the doctor in this book to indicate that he wants his servants or guards to make haste and obey his orders.

Hirsute. A word that means hairy, and one that should be used very rarely, as it is a little too scientific.

Hold. In this book, the word is used in speaking of a boat, or the part of a vessel below the deck.

Hold. In this book, the word is used in speaking of a boat, or the part of a vessel below the deck.

Hold Out. To persevere.

Hold Your Tongue. To be silent; a command often given by the doctor's wife in this book.

Home. A word that is used by all to indicate their birthplace, or the place where they are living, and where they want to return to; but in the tropics, the term "home" often has a very special meaning, as it indicates that the individual referred to has a wife waiting for him; and it may be added, that often this word "home" is used to denote a house and grounds with a good garden and an abundance of everything that money can buy, for the idea is that everyone, sooner or later, wants to get back to the comfort and luxury of his home.

Honied. A term that signifies very sweet, as it would be the honey made by bees; but it can also be used in speaking of words or deeds, or even looks, that are intended to persuade or deceive.

Hookah. A pipe, used in the East for smoking.

Hot. A term used in this book to indicate the intense heat of the tropical sun; and one that is a constant discomfort to the inhabitants, especially when they are in a state of excitement.

Hot-roll. A name invented by the author of this book to indicate that a man was fond of new bread; but it is a name that could only be given to a man who is known for his simple tastes.

House. A building in which people live, and it might be added, one that is supposed by the author to be much more desirable in the tropics than a *hut*.

Humph. A term that is used to express a feeling of doubt or displeasure.

Hussar. A kind of cavalry soldier, whose uniform is very showy. The Sultan Murad in this book is very fond of hussar uniforms, but he has never been able to obtain one that fits him.

I. In this book, the author uses the term "I"

Timeline

The Reverend Arthur Rosebury is visited by Dr. Bolter, who will act as an escort for two young women he will meet along the way.

Dr. Bolter finds out about Miss Rosebury's troubles, and how he helped her brother in the past.

Miss Twettenham reprimands Helen Perowne, the most beautiful pupil at the Firlawns school, for her "coquetry".

Dr. Bolter visits Miss Twettenham's, and meets the two young women, Helen Perowne and Grey Stuart.

Miss Twettenham faints after discovering a note attached to a stone thrown over the garden wall.

Dr. Bolter takes note of the beauty of Helen Perowne.

The two young women are invited to the Rectory. Helen Perowne asks the Reverend Arthur to show her the garden.

Dr. Bolter proposes to Miss Rosebury.

Miss Rosebury explains her refusal, which is based on her desire to not leave her brother.

Dr. Bolter mentions the vacant chaplaincy at Sindang to Arthur Rosebury.

The Reverend Arthur Rosebury agrees to go to Sindang with Dr. Bolter and Miss Rosebury.

The journey to Sindang starts.

Helen Perowne and Grey Stuart are introduced to the other residents at the station.

Dr. Bolter shares his theory about the location of Solomon's Ophir.

Helen Perowne and her father host a dinner party.

Murad, the Rajah, proposes to Helen Perowne.

Helen Perowne locks herself in her room to avoid Murad.

The Rajah angrily leaves Mr. Perowne's home.

The Inche Maida, a neighboring princess, comes to the

Residency island to appeal for help from the British residents.

Dr. Bolter and Mrs. Bolter discuss Helen Perowne's behavior.

Helen Perowne and Grey Stuart have a conversation in their room.

Helen Perowne notices that Dr. Bolter and Miss Rosebury are quite close.

Dr. Bolter proposes to Miss Rosebury again, and she accepts.

Murad visits the Residency island to ask for help with the Inche Maida's case, and proposes an evening gathering for the residents.

Dr. Bolter goes on an expedition into the interior.

Chumbley tells Mrs. Bolter about Helen Perowne's behavior.

Dr. Bolter returns from his expedition and proposes a move to Sindang, suggesting that Arthur Rosebury accept the vacant chaplaincy there.

Arthur Rosebury agrees to go to Sindang.

The group embarks on their journey to Sindang.

Helen Perowne tries to pique Neil Harley by flirting with other men.

The group arrives at Sindang.

Rajah Murad begins to visit Mr. Perowne frequently.

Rajah Murad proposes to Helen Perowne.

The Inche Maida comes to the Residency island to ask the British residents to help her with her problems.

Dr. Bolter makes another expedition into the interior.

Helen Perowne and Grey Stuart have a conversation in their room.

The Inche Maida hosts a feast for the English residents, where Helen Perowne and Captain Hilton flirt with each other.

Murad and the Inche Maida seem to become jealous of Helen Perowne and Captain Hilton, respectively.

The Inche Maida invites the English residents for a trip up the river.

The Rajah, Captain Hilton, and Chumbley are taken prisoner.

Murad takes Helen Perowne prisoner.

Dr. Bolter, Mrs. Bolter, and Arthur Rosebury begin searching for the missing.

The search reveals that the missing were taken by the Malays.

Rajah Murad comes to Mr. Perowne's home and faints upon hearing of Helen Perowne's disappearance.

The Inche Maida visits Mr. Perowne's home and offers her help.

The search continues, and a boat, which is believed to have been involved in a crocodile attack, is discovered.

The residents begin to suspect that Murad was responsible for the abduction.

Helen Perowne wakes up in the Rajah's home and learns that her face and teeth have been altered to resemble a Malay woman.

The Reverend Arthur Rosebury wakes up in a prison in the jungle and begins to study plants.

The prisoners, Captain Hilton and Chumbley, are visited by the Inche Maida.

The Rajah visits Helen Perowne and explains his motives.

Helen Perowne tries to escape.

Helen Perowne is visited by the Malay girl who helped her escape.

Dr. Bolter goes on an expedition up a river to find Helen Perowne.

Helen Perowne and the Malay girl attempt to escape.

Helen Perowne and the Malay girl are recaptured.

The Malay girl is taken away and Helen Perowne is visited by Murad's wives.

Helen Perowne is disfigured further by the wives of Murad.

The Malay girl helps Helen Perowne escape again.

The two women are chased by the Rajah's men and a tiger.

The men, Chumbley and Hilton, escape from their prison by breaking through the bamboo floor.

The Inche Maida visits the prisoners and proposes a deal to Hilton.

Murad visits Helen Perowne again.

Helen Perowne attempts to escape, and is recaptured.

Murad attempts to kiss Helen Perowne, and she strikes him in the face.

Murad falls into a stupor after drinking poisoned wine.

Helen Perowne escapes from her prison, but is recaptured by the Rajah's women.

Helen Perowne is visited by the Malay girl who helped her escape, and they attempt to escape again.

Helen Perowne falls from the roof and is helped by the Malay girl.

The two women are pursued by the Rajah's men and a tiger.

The men, Chumbley and Hilton, escape from the Rajah's home.

A Malay messenger comes to the Residency island with a message from the Inche Maida, informing them that Helen is being held prisoner by the Rajah.

The boat carrying the Malay messenger is overtaken by Murad's men.

The Resident organizes a search party and prepares the Residency island for a possible attack by the Malays.

The search party finds a boat that is believed to have been attacked by crocodiles.

The residents start to suspect that Murad is behind the abductions.

The Rajah arrives at the Residency and faints after learning of Helen Perowne's disappearance.

The residents debate about their next step, and finally decide to search Murad's home.

Dr. Bolter goes to Mr. Perowne's home to help with the search, and is interrupted by Mrs. Barlow.

The search party visits the doctor's home, and learns that Hilton and Chumbley were missing.

The Malay messenger who informed the Resident of Helen Perowne's whereabouts is questioned.

Murad escapes from prison and runs amok through the streets of Singapore, killing several people.

Captain Hilton is wounded by Murad while trying to help the people.

Murad is killed by a spear thrown at him by a policeman.

Captain Hilton and Chumbley are released, and return to Sindang.

The Malay messenger is released.

The residents continue to search for the chaplain.

Dr. Bolter, Mrs. Bolter, and Grey Stuart nurse Helen Perowne back to health.

Murad is sent to Singapore to stand trial.

The Residents receive a message from Helen Perowne, who is very ill and wants to see Neil Harley.

Neil Harley visits Helen, and she tells him that she wants him to forgive her.

Helen Perowne dies.

The Rajah is found dead in prison after he escapes from the island and runs amok.

Dr. Bolter, Mrs. Bolter, and Arthur Rosebury return to England.

Grey Stuart marries Captain Hilton.

Chumbley marries the Inche Maida.

The Inche Maida becomes a Rajah and rules Campong Selah.

Neil Harley comes to England for a year's leave.

Helen Perowne's family receives word that he is coming to Paris and will be staying at a specific hotel.

The story concludes with the Hiltons happily settled in England.

Milton Keynes UK
Ingram Content Group UK Ltd.
UKHW020104181024
449757UK00012B/714

9 781608 883424